Unsung Words From a Wonderful Us

Poems by

Samuel Ezra

Unsung Words From a Wonderful Us

ISBN: 9798644774531

Original cover artwork by Sophie Ferch

Contents

Song 4

Song 5

Song 6

Song 7

Song 8

Beautifully Lost

Sat with my sweating
best friend Moretti on this concrete stair
that looks towards the fiery sea of Sicily
I feel like a fly.

A group of teens sit victoriously
in the winter sun before me,
the boys run fingers through their partner's hair
engraving their bodies on the daydreaming grass,
lost in the chalk outline of young love.

On the 7th step
to my left
sits a leather skinned man in a
flat cap
much like my Grandad's,
his eyes are drowned in defeat
staring at the eroding bricks of
this and
his theatre,
slouched like a fly without flight.

I wonder if he too once ran his fingers through
the hair of a woman,
if he once wore that same smile inside
and bathed in young love beneath a
naked southern sky.

His old wings have grown with rust,
life's winter has been tough
and

taken its toll on his school-day skin,
what's strange is knowing
one day we'll sit just like him

in the sun on a Sunday

beautifully lost.

Song to my City

She is the drunken princess

Her stubborn waves
wash onto a
bay of boozers
and cigarette butts,
chiseled cliffs
and
Friday night fisticuffs.

She's my kind of ugly.

Becoming

I remember watching my father
shave as a child,
gently stroking his face
with the razor's edge
while I watched on,
wondering when I too would become a man.

That day came around my
15th year on Earth,
I loaded the weapon,
added the foam
and looked into the eyes
of the child staring back.

The first swipe took some skin,
as blood spilled down my face
I stopped and watched
the river of my childhood
drip and drain into that sink,

I tried to fish out the dreams as they faded
into old-age balloons before me,
but the bait was weak.

Sadly and swiftly

I became this man.

Twin Town

If Swansea were a food,
it would be the mayonnaise slapped
on a Friday night kebab,
being eaten by boys dressed as Britney
on a fancy-dress stag.

If Swansea were a singer,
it would be the electricity that runs a karaoke
machine,
being run by a guy called Dai
who knows every word
to every song by Queen.

If Swansea were a sport,
she would be a 30 man brawl in a rugby match,
and the day after the whole city
would talk about who was the 'ardest man on the
grass.

If Swansea were a car,
it would have been nicked a long time ago
joyriding round the world
fuelled by a crate of mixed berries 'bow

If Swansea was a comedian,
she'd be out doing stand up in the never-ending
rain
and if disaster struck,
she'd neck a pint, laugh, and hit the stage again.

If my city was perfect,

I'd immediately divorce myself from her side,

this lovely, ugly city
makes an ugly, lovely bride.

A Swansea Love Story

I once woke up so drunk
that 2pac was back alive
Swansea had won the FA cup
and my girlfriend loved me.

A few hours later,
to see if I was sober
I called my girlfriend
and told her I loved her too
'What's wrong with 'ew?' was her reply.

I ended the call,
headed to the fridge,
and began to make her love me once again.

City by the Sea

My teen years were spent in front of a furnace,
9 years of melting away the child
while Swansea multiplied my sins.
Dylan's city of broken ambition
held true to its roots for me,
surrounded by paper flowers
whose petals withered away
beside the crushing Welsh waves.

Scarred knuckles from
the splash of molten metal,
darkened fields from the crash
of a family tree,
society drank away the pain
of routine, and this daydreaming teen
did the same, growing fluent in the language of
livers,
no one to tell me different
or friend who knew of freedom,
the city sucked me in.

The city where dreams come to die, and everyone
sits in the rain and drinks,
waving
them
goodbye.

3:04 a.m.

Being awake
while the madness rests
ignites the scent of life.
No traffic or
chatting to fence the
broken beauty,
3.04 am raindrops
patter on the tiles,
beating out a hollow song
that warms this
grown child's bones.

Not a light is awake along the row
of giant sleeping faces
who gently puff cigars
into the Swansea air.
The stars that will be
starved in years
are feasting tonight,
alive and shining at 3.04 on a
Wednesday
mourning.

So much to do in this hamster cage
whose wheel has rusted tight,
a lonely harmonica
a weeping guitar
a half written poem
that mumbles
empty nothings in the mind.
The silence.

The safety.
The leaking sky.

No problems exist around this time,
just me and my window to a
one street world
and the feeling that out there,
somewhere,
is
so
much
more.

Be the Wave

I pushed
pause on a
podcast this morning
as a scientist explained
how the same
water that makes 60% of your body work
was once condensing into clouds
somewhere out
in the Indian ocean,
raining down into the Himalayas,
rushing into the Ganges and
back towards the sea where it was born.

Is this why whenever I look out at the ocean,
I see so much more than water.

One day I'll follow

I opened my pad hoping for inspiration
on an uninspired Swansea day

when 3 pigeons came and sat by my side.
Bodies wobbling as they made their way to my
words, I could see one wearing a sadness in his
eyes, watching the robots walk to work, slaves to a
wage,

the bittersweet symphony which Ashcroft played.

I tell him I'm jealous of his wings
as he tilts his neck and strains to understand,
maybe words aren't enough.

I look up at the sky and he looks with me,
stepping towards the edge of the bench
he takes off to the clouds,
leaving me,

my words

and Swansea behind

Sleeping on the seats at Heathrow

A silence that taps
like a mouse
in an empty opera
house,
a refreshment stand blinks
and sits alone,
surrounded by suitcase eyes
trying to close.

Its chamber music to butterflies,
a place that thrives
with strangers' lives
most of the time
just dreams and dies
at night.

I guess even giants need rest.

My eyes close to the sounds of a
brush beneath my bench,
a brush that sweeps away my past
as I look towards the oval glow on the ceiling,
the patter of feet fades away
until all that is left
is me
and this terminal of
tiger-like tenderness.

I dip my tongue inside
the silence and drink the moment.

In the morning
life will
rush through this place,
a river without rules

but for now
she sleeps,

allowing her 4 walls
to close their weary eyes and
softly
snore
with London's
dying
stars.

Song to a second home

She is the breathing oxymoron.

The singing of her satay smoke,
the rush of her wheels
and purr of her lights.

Friday skyscrapers
and
Monday bridges.

She is the homeless throne
to a princess with charcoal hair.

How did that happen?

I fell asleep in Swansea and
woke up lost in front of an
Indonesian whiteboard.
41 faces looking up at me for answers
to questions I held myself,
I answered with laughs and they
responded with smiles,
my weekdays became weekends
thanks to the friendly faces
inside those four walls,
inviting me into their lives
and reminding me how good
it feels to live like
there's no gravestone
waiting.

On my last day
they each made me a
gift on paper as a reminder of our time.

I look back at those poems and pictures now
and realise I was the student
in that classroom.
My 41 teachers taught me
that maybe I'd found something
I truly loved.

9 years on,
sat in this teacher's office
writing these very words,
I feel every one of them

deserves a poem
which says a simple,
but life-defining

Thank you.

Under a Bridge

They sat beneath a dirty Jakarta sun,
a grandmother
a girl
a glimmering can of
Coke.

The grandmother took a short sip
then passed it to the girl
who lay as softly as
a sleeping sonnet
on her lap.

As the girl held the can with both hands
and slowly took her meal for the day,
I saw that same Jakarta sun
glisten in the
Grandmother's eyes.

Life begins at the lights

Two weeks in to my first teaching job
I bought a vespa from a student,
he lived on the East of the city
while home to me was the West.

In Wales that's 20 minutes on a bicycle,
in Jakarta that's 2 hours of chewing air and
digesting petrol.

I'd never driven before,
I thought a city of 10 million people
and 15 million motorbikes was the best place to
begin.

I pulled up at my first traffic light,
as the drivers either side
smiled at the alien between them,
pointing forwards
wanting to race
as the red face
counted down.

Red
Blue (Indonesians don't do amber) … Green

Note to reader: (Please choose your ending)

Ending 1

I turned the throttle

on the machine and
took off along the runway before me,
as I raced into the distance
I looked back at the drivers
and saw them choking in the
smoke of my victory.

Ending 2 a.k.a The Truth

I turned the throttle on the machine and
did nothing like take off along the runway before
me. I sat there confused with this handle and that
pedal but then …

those same smiles who had been either side came
back and started my engine,

we drove off into the city together and

I started to understand why I was here.

How to eat your way into my heart …

For our first date
you took me for a bowl of chicken feet
in a tent disguised as a shop
by the side of a city street.
I watched you chew the flesh in seconds
and spit the bones with the accuracy of
an acrobat
back onto the plate.

20 something feet
gone
in 20 something minutes.

We jumped back into your car,
rolled down the windows
and tuned into the radio waves
of the city at midnight.

As we drove between the
sleeping giants of Jakarta
I thought of those poor fowl corpses you had
left lying there
heaped quietly on that plate
like the remnants of
a baby elephant's graveyard

and I felt
the shield inside me
drop.

… and How to break it

I sit beside the window
trying to escape the goodbye,
watching you wash dishes
for the last time.

The shadowed valley falls silent
the choking cars no longer rush,
the pool beneath your window
sits and weeps its walls over us.

We lived and loved over temple
bells and Islamic calls to prayer,
but now we sit in this empty, white space
with our future in the air.

The furniture has left, along with
the midnight hugs,
the suitcase packed the clothes and socks
but forgot to take the love.

I sit beside that window
for a second every day,
watching you wash those dishes
watching,
wishing,
I had stayed.

The Clipping of my Wings

As the Orange Oval sinks into its lone and lucid
ocean, the voice over the rusty tannoy reads the
gate is open. We sit over a muffin and a plate of
empty plans,
    although It's you that takes the flight, I've no
idea where I'll land.
        3 years
         of living life like
          free-birds
          we dipped inside a
           dream world
            slid down rainbows
            feet first
             that Honda Jazz's
             wheels burst
              it felt like we could
              leave earth
               we loved, we laughed
                and we hurt,
                  but everything
must stop.

And here we sit over a
muffin and a plate of empty plans
as you stand up to board the flight
I've no idea where I'll
land.

Tana Toraja

There's a small village
tucked away in the middle
of the 'K' that is
Sulawesi.

There, a dead father
sits on the same sofa
as his living wife,
his eyes sink into his skull
as his embalmed arms
sleep by his side.

The cost of entry to a traveller
like me, is a pack of cigarettes
placed on the father's lap
and a firm belief that there is still life
inside that much death.

As I handed my cigarettes to the corpse,
I looked into where his eyes once lived
and I truly did feel something breath inside
that room.

I left the village the next day,
but that man has never left me.

The Ghost of Chinatown

Cross legged on the
cracked tiles
level with the rats,
but not a rat,
a rat's got more panache,
more passion
more zest
he sits
stone dead.
Waiting...
staring...
nothing.
Tomorrow it'll rain,
tomorrow will be today all over again.
He'll sit cross legged, level with that rats
sucking tasteless water from a torn plastic bag,
as passers-by
walk by his side
he wonders if he's even
really there?

The moon revolves around the Earth
The Earth revolves around the Sun

but he just sits
cross legged

level with the rats.

Bali Marathon

'Welcome to Bali' the children chant
as their purple sun seeps from
beneath its grass bed,
the Giant AGUNG awakes in the distance,
its rocky eye bleeds the padi-fields
a blood red.

Pots of rainbows, thrown on roads
filled with potholes,
leave a trail of Lavender that
feeds breathless nostrils.
Demon masks dance; purple incense burns,
road signs read like broken
alphabet spaghetti words.

Satay smoke flirts with the day's first mosquitoes,
banana trees glow a golden green in the haze,
high fives and smiles are passed around
like cheap halos
as joy swims down the sweat of every runner's face.

Women as old as oak sew their seeds in straw hats,
looking strangely at the white skinned
aliens racing past.
My legs grew sore but their smiles did not
with a playground like this the biggest
challenge is to stop …

Peter Pan at 30

It was a Saturday,
school had just closed its doors
and we walked out to find a trolley
resting on the road.

My friend looked at me
and my eyes answered 'yes',
I hopped into the trolley
as he began pushing me back towards
my childhood.

Passers by began to cheer
at the 30 year-old Peter Pan
in school shirt and shoes
racing towards the unknown.

As I hit the curb
and took for the skies
the city laughed beside me.

I landed beneath a palm tree,
accepted the applause of my audience,
stood up,
and there was
a student of mine
with eyes that said

'I might not go on Monday'

The Homeless Saxophonist

Fingers cloaked in smoked leather skin
play the pain of each
punctured hymn,
each bruised note floats with rusty wings
as his saxophone sings a lost song.

King to the subway; rat to the rest,
a bible of stories stored in his flesh,
each note rolls out of the dark
undressed,
as his saxophone sings 'life's been long.'

Lost in the music, both broken eyes shut,
holds hope for a rattle from his plastic cup,
a tilt of the head is his thanks very much
as his saxophone sings a lost song.

I wonder what scraped the gold from his bones,
when fields were still green
could he bleed those same notes,
it seems age is sandpaper
that carves our life's roads,
I hear a lifetime of loss
through that old saxophone.

Song to the Rising Sun

She is the calm before the quiet

Silence is her soundtrack.
The footsteps of snowflakes
dance on the stage of
her skin.
She is the actress
and the audience,
the poet
and the poem.

She is Japan

年を取る

There's a corner of the park
where grown men meet,
speaking on grass beds
in words only the world
beneath them hears.

A Spring symphony of
smoke and
broken smiles.

Their shoes beside them as
they fill their lungs with liquor,
removing their skin for a splash
of Japanese sun as
newspapers in their hands
catch the
ash of their day.

A soft, rushing water
whispers behind them
as their words take a new wind.
A young girl,
barely 6
walks
alongside
the
stream
of
their
cigarettes,

kneels amongst the pigeons
with a handful of bread,
while the men sew up their skin
to stop their clocks
and watch.
Their smiles speak
an ageing tale
as the girl feeds
the feathered birds,
generations between
them
but the same skin that
kisses the grass of spring,
growing old together
in their own special way,
in the corner of a park,
tucked away
in a corner

of the world.

Found on a mountain

We Climbed Fuji,
two fools
no flashlight
no food
no gloves
no guide
no map
no mind
but man...
SUNRISE,
worth every frozen finger
every icy rock climbed,
the perfect burning purple
smoke
to hide from our lives

GIANTS
above the clouds

Sometimes I wish
we
never
came
down.

What does she keep in that coffee?

Why does she sit alone behind
that coffee shop window,
slowly stirring her
dying cup while
the Tokyo rain sings
its final hymn?

The last words of an ageing poet
are painted in charcoal
beneath her eyes,
it seems life
is in its taking stage
and she's been
robbed of it all,
gently stirring inside her paper cup
as the rain falls.

Alone,
behind her misty
window
to a
world made of
fading metaphors.

Haruki told a lie

I always thought I'd fall in love
in a Japanese jazz bar
just like they do in his books.

The first time I stepped inside
the door of such a place
I was greeted by a tsunami of cigar smoke,
a man painting sick on his barstool
and a row of women who charged by the hour.

So feel free to believe in a future
but never, ever pin YOUR dreams
on the
dreams
of Murakami.

The Most Beautiful Death in Japan

A cherry blossom
is the perfect Haiku,
Life and death
in a sky of syllables,
Beauty washed away
into a bare branch of forgotten
muscle,
As fragile as the
skin of a
Snail.

These forests age
much like me and you.

Time reveals the worn-out bones
that bore
the weight of this world.

Blossoms dance
their final notes
beside a log long forgotten
by the passing feet,
that
unknowingly sweep
through its sea
of
dying petals.

Admiring the youth of the year
as they catch the wind

and get washed away to the
Jagged grave
below.

Dying a beautiful death
in a silence as sharp as
the beheading
of a feather,

leaving me up here with
the living,
wondering
how everything
I love
will
sing that final
song.

A White Year of Silence

We spent the year among the mountains,
quiet roads wrapped around
our tatami floor
as we wrapped around each other,
hugging beneath a stranded roof,
hiding from the white of winter.

Every corner of the town was ours
the riverside our weekend bed
as the alps played the violin
to the soundtrack of our steps.

Sushi picnics, green tea bottles
Sapporo cans and castles,
Sundays we'd take the lonely trains
that ran through Japan's shadows.

Wandering trails through seas of trees
to slow sunsets on powdered peaks
while Tokyo's lights would shine and speed
we'd sit and watch our
castle sleep.

Then cherry blossoms came and
waved goodbye the long winter
I felt the warmth of spring
beneath the clutching of our fingers.

You painted smiles on faces
of a classroom full of kids
who looked up to their teacher
for the creative soul she is.

A yoga mat rolled out and breathed
new life into your days,
I watched you through the mirror
wear a new smile on your face.

We closed that door one last time
kissed the paper walls goodnight
on days spent in the beauty
of a solitary life.

Some nights it felt like only you and I
existed here,
walking hand in hand
beside the silence
of the year.

Our Japanese Castle

Matsumoto-jo
asleep on a lake of life
the swans and stars cry.

Her tiles tilt like tears
streaming from a samurai sky
frosted home of old.

A full moon watches
her reflection glaze the water
poem in the lake.

A Gift from Kim

Nothing says 'I'm alive' more
than laying on a tatami mat

while a North Korean missile
fires overhead on a Friday morning.

.

Jagged Dreamer

Life
is never
lived more fully
than at the peak of a mountain.
Tickling the sky with your sweat and sacrifice.

Looking
through the eyes
of a child at the unearthly smoke
dancing around the wrinkled cheeks of god.
Dressed in snow and a supernatural silence that
secretly whispers all the unknown wonders of us.

They
are the real sleeping
giants of childhood dreams
igniting the flames of what life has been,
weaving the ambition of what can become,
when you realise what can be reached from the
bottom.

Sleep well

Did I know you more or less
than I thought?
A smile and a touch of the shoulder
is the most I can remember,
but those are enough.

Footprints of early friendship.

The sun came out shining
when you set too soon,
a fragment of a memory still
sits on that park bench in Osaka,
sipping Asahi
laughing through our night.

More than just faces you meet,
they are pieces of a defeated
jigsaw that sift through time

while we try and make sense of the
unsensible.

Knowing that we had those
moments and memories
is sometimes the only sense there is.

Sleep well my friend.

Akashi

From a Shinkansen window
our eyes meet.

A smile is shared
that speaks of the mystery of
this human condition

the quest for self
and the meaning of this
skin and sin.

Life in seconds.

Love in the blink of a platform.

Word rich stares through a window
that weave a language of life.

I hope the journey goes well,

Stranger.

Lover.

Friend.

Out there somewhere

Lost at sea
on a ship
whose wood has slowly
rotted away,
whose walls have been
breached by the waves of
old age.

She sits and fills her bucket
with the salty water of her tears.

Emptying the boat,
preserving the life
that lies within,
deafened by that
rushing wind.
She hears little
but feels with the sense
of a skydiver
with no shoot.

Alone in a boat
since he swam ashore
and chose
to live on different sands.

Aimless days
with blunted darts
thrown at midnight boards.
Sometimes it feels like the
boat I once knew

and watched
in oar
just sits afloat and afraid,
conserving the ageing of the days
on the bed of that silent,
sanguine
sea.

Song to the Sun

She is the drummer of our days

Sat behind her hi-hat,
keeping rhythm with the flow
of our footsteps
and the beating of
our fears.

She is ours.

I Miss That Swing

Another park bench,
me,
the Sicilian air
and this paper.
A woman pushes her young son lovingly
on a swing
as he screams and chuckles with joy
at every push.
They have no worries of
the world
debts or
jobs,
just love,
untouched by the daggers of time.
The beauty of watching
how warmly
this mother takes her son by the hand
and guides him through the park
makes my pen begin to paint.
People spend their whole life in
search of such grace,
at the peak of mountains,
from the windows of planes,
in women,
in men.

But the beauty of a mother's love
is beyond any words
any poet
could ever pen

So I
Stop

Sit

and
watch.

One of those moments when Jimi plays

While the early year sun
beats down on the step where we sit,
the world begins to wake around us.
Sounds of Andalusia wash the lake above
with notes that remind you
Africa is a staircase away
while the mountains remind you
that man is an ant on the
tail of a tiger.

A cat steps around the stones
in search of something
even she doesn't understand.

Is it love?
That 4 letter word that washes ashore,
unexpected
to dance on your sand
while the winds rage around you.

Or is it life?
The ability to have seen that love bleed and burn,
and still be willing to let it breathe again,
the same life I feel as I look towards the
limestone mystery in the distance.

As the music of life plays around us
I think of the lost questions that beat the drum
of every cloud in the sky.
I'm not sure whether it is for love or for life
but here on this step today

I feel Jimi play inside,

I am truly alive.

Green but Blue

Morning walk through a Sicilian park
with daylight in full swing,
the greens and blues of life all dance
in winter's gentle wind,

when you enter my head
forgotten friend, forever young,
whose blues and greens were lost
before the painting had begun.

I see you in your Swansea scarf,
all hope on that green pitch,
telling us how you could score the
chance that Trundle missed.

A missed phone call I still regret
I didn't see the storm,
this city by the sea woke up to find
that you'd moved on.

The circus lost its main act,
hundreds lost a friend,
the tears of the clown brought
his performance to an end,

morning walk through a Sicilian park
with daylight in full swing
and how I wish you sat beside me on this bench
to take it in.

A mourning he'd love

The white-washed walls of Seville
wake slowly
between the yawning sun and the fading moon.
As the birds begin their daily dance,
dropping in circles at the thrill of another day
the Giralda and her cream skin
sit in the morning's shadow,
a reminder of a time forgotten.

My family asleep in their beds,
safe from the outside
and any sense of
an end.
But as the air grows warmer
something feels missing.

Someone.

These were moments he'd love,
watching the world take a new breath
beside us.
Looking out across the beauty of Seville
on this Saturday
reminds me of the love
and loss that comes with
living.

The soundtrack to being human.

The true theme tune to being alive.

To the Spanish seagull who stole my sandwich

I may not know who you are
but I know what you look like.

I'm pretty sure I just saw your cousin
so I told him to pass this message on to you
and your husband.

'If I don't wake up to 3 euros
or a fully furnished
prawn mayo meal deal sandwich
by Monday
I'm making the first move'

and actually,
I'm charging interest.
I expect
some sea salt kettle crisps
and a can of Pepsi with a lemon twist
or else I'm coming up there to your ends
with 2 steaming, swinging fists.

You mugged the wrong man,
the morals of Vin Diesel's streets are the
morals of my skies.

Go hard or go home. Ride or Die.
It's me and you to the grave
my feathery friend.

Wu-Tang raised me.
The first time the razor clipped
my adult cheek,
the Rza was living in my
headphone home.

The drumbeat of my late teenage days
was beaten to the sound
of jagged footsteps
echoing through
36 chambers.
Hip Hop let me grow.

The crackle and hiss of a
troublesome twenties
played out beside cheap kung fu samples
and Tesco milk crates filled with 2nd hand vinyls.

Hip hop was a friend
I turned to on those first nights away from home
when I searched for some comfort
surrounding myself in voices that
I know.

My neighbour on bus rides,
the bible ink on my chest,
the first time my heart got broken
I turned to Mos Def.

Every step I took along that road

from teen until today,
was taken with a head nod
as the drums just played
and play …

I wish those flowers didn't grow

I don't carry much in that rucksack except my life.
Four years of hole filled socks, faces and names.

Some I've forgotten, but most still sit on a bench
somewhere between my Sunday morning brain
and my Friday night liver.

Some are as fresh as the skin of a lemon,
growing on trees in my mind that I choose to never
prune.

They helped grow the perfect garden, gave me days
that made the nights rage with envy, and nights
that made the days taste as dry as a desert.

Though the two fruits that linger the most are
there, laid beneath that bridge,

one the size of a mother,

the other the size of her daughter,
.
sleeping or dying?
I'll never know.

But there they sit and grow in that
same garden in my mind.

It all begins with a scissors

There's a man who sits on the street
in Seville, cutting empty cans into
animal shapes
he can sell.

His only tool is a scissors,
a cut here
a slice there
and the meaningless
becomes the meaningful.

Most of us have a scissors
somewhere in the kitchen
or hidden in the drawer of our futures.

Maybe today is a good day
to make that first cut.

Song to the Unexpected

She is every noun in the dictionary.

Her colours and chaos
are splashed across the
train-tracks
of her skin.

She is anarchy and affection,
the ghost and the graffiti

Smiles often sit next to you on Indian buses

A simple cup of Chai,
milk and spice
and a sprinkle of kindness
passed through the bus window
towards my thirsty lips.
5 rupees from an empty wallet
that knows no depth
to generosity.
It's amazing what a drink can do,
filling the lonely lines
in my stomach
and bringing together
2 strangers

riding the road of dust to
nowhere,
sharing
a cup of chai
and a smile.

Beside The Ganges

The green lifeblood of India flows like molten ice
as life grows beside.
Saddhus sit and spoon dahl
into lips hid beneath their frosty beards,
white skinned worshippers
sit in the lotus
and look towards the light
in a land like no other.
A local in sari
dips her feet in the
deep green snake
and swims as her spirit
is cleansed,
horns hang on the bow shaped bridge
as engines sing a
ca-cough-ony of hymns.

Beside me sits a man in peace,
his feet caked with that same life,
those same sounds
and same scars.
His cigarette burns as slow as
The great Ganges glides.

Up   and   out   into   the
waiting   sky

That sits and watches the
Padma and the life that lives beside.

Triveni Ghat

As a group of boys play with
broken bike tyres
bouncing them along the ghats,
I think of all I have.

Spoiled by geography
for shelter and shoes
while some have only
their skin
their sanity
and maybe,
if they are lucky,

a broken bike tyre.

If you can, sit on the roof

If you want to know what a rough night
on an Indian bus sounds like
please, close your eyes …

Imagine all windows rusted shut
Imagine a seat which doesn't stay up,
Imagine that seat continuously falling back
onto a large Indian woman
who greets every movement of
that seat throughout the night with a slap.

Now, imagine a 13-hour ride
through a 35 degree night
trying to hold that seat up high
to avoid the swing of that woman's palm
and catch some shut eye.

That pretty much sums up the last 200 miles.

View From The Hub

Midnight on a squeaky mattress
surrounded by
drying socks,
thinking how it all went right
the day I chose to go get lost.

My window peers out to a
drunk who waves
and yells at cars.
If they don't park
he doesn't eat,
If he doesn't eat
I don't sleep,
the gin and the yang.

It's a world away
yet not a shoeprint far
from the window
where I watched
Swansea slither by
through the same sunken eyes.

Broken phone boxes
and drunken fights became
eyes that sought answers
and words that sought life.

Nights of vices
and mornings of broken breath
became days of meeting strangers

climbing stairs of happiness.

So as those socks dry above my bed,
I think of the skin I left on the washing line of my
youth,
and the rucksack by my side filled
with a future
                          I can choose.

Dharamsala

Today I woke
with the pieces of my mind
aligned and
fixed
like the fist
of a spider.

Tibetan prayer flags and
rushing glaciers race through the minutes
in my mind.
Six years old again,
rock hopping
hop rocking
in afternoon shadows
with strangers turned friends.

These are my days

writing by rock pools
painting tales
on Himalayan canvases.
Tasting and embracing the poverty of existence
and the richness of just being.
Days like this are why we take
the road
from home
and search for answers to the great
unknown.

We dance to the top of the mountain,
take 3 sharp breaths,

3 animated steps

and there is Tibet

Standing in all its
gracious glory.

Not Many Words Needed For The Taj Mahal

A whole building built from love
a teardrop of time.
Death and life in marble walls
painted on a
pulse of
sky.

Song to the balloon with no helium

She is forever flying then falling.

Even when she feels safe in my hands
I know the helium is limited
and the drop will come.

She is the best and the worst
the carrot cake and the curse.

She is …

My Broken Parachute

I once fell in love
for 5 minutes.
Her eyes of the finest
black marble
and spirit of scarlet flames
cocooned around that
Malaysian day,
selotaping the broken string
of my three-year parachute,
through the storm
and into her.

Chinatown's muddy stone streets
told secrets beneath our sandals
as we spoke in broken words.
A quiet drink in a crowded place
then a cold walk to the station
a swift embrace
and
she was gone.

My parachute string snapped
once more
as the ground opened up
preparing to
catch me

once

again

Do They Still Make Love Like This?

Walking along that hospital
tunnel towards a room
where lives are decided,
I watch my Grandfather
stride proudly
with cane in hand
towards a door of
questions,
an aged man with the eyes of a child.

I see him prepared for the worst
as he looks into the tunnel,
the lights of the room flicker
in the distance,
but a light in this room
ignites the moment,
as the fingers that have lived beside him for
most of his life
take him by the hand
and softly say without words
that

everything will be okay.

Quarantine Life with You (for Sophie)

I wake you up to the coffee song
as you lay there and the sun plays
Saturday cinema with your hair,
flaunting its freedom
on our pillow.

Eyes I've swam inside
for 5 years worth
of mornings
start my day with
the unspoken song of a
hummingbird.

We roll out Yoga mats,
I stumble like a
drunken dinosaur as
you move with the elegance of
a tarantula on a tightrope.
The waterfall of my sweat
drops its last salt
as we escape the
bars of our bedroom
and head out towards
somewhere only we know.

2 metres between us and the world
but the waist of a cigarette paper
couldn't fit between our fingers
while we walk through
streets as silent as a circus
in a cemetery.

We watch the moon
climb to claim its halo for the night
and as silence falls over the gardens
of unsung harmonies,
we lay together
and
dream of our wings.

Unspoken

The momentous moments of my life
were never caught
in a picture
or a tweet.
My best times were between
me and the moon.

Timeless and untainted

sometimes sweeping back
unexpectedly.

A smell
A song
The sea.

They are my moments
never put to paper
or permitted to leave the lips.

A secret with the stars
and those eyes that watch from
behind the clouds.

Analog Love of a Mother in Myanmar

I sat and watched this bronze Burmese mother
and her daughter while sat on a log
in the October sun.
A thatched straw roof over their heads and
dried out vegetable patch out front.

No electricity
No i-pods
No i-pads

Just eyes

eyes that were
infinitely filled
with a mother's love.

One Last

Will there be one last letter
between the setting sun
and the rising moon?
A selection of words
to let him hear that the
waves had calmed too soon.

Will there be one last poem
to express the extent
of our time?
Hand in hand through the world
we walked
with words too deep
for a line.

Will there be one last song
on a guitar
whose strings have turned to rust?
Every swing of the plectrum
sweeps the sea
in search of signs
of us.

Will there be one last mountain
a viewpoint to
look at our lives,
to see how we've gone
from lovers to strangers
in only the
blink of an eye.

The Dying Light

She painted a paper smile
on the wings of a fading wave,
lost at sea
like a wingless bird and her
world doesn't spin the same.

She says she's looking for something,
a light that's been out for years,
swimming out towards a sea of escape
while our coastline disappears.

The more you say goodbye
The stronger the dying light grows.

The more time passes by
The bonfire flickers and glows.

Let me be
The light that shines for you.

Please. Please, Please let me be
The light that shines for you.

The Greatest Adventure I Never Had

I woke up from a dream
of you

one night spent lost

a lifetime found

I wonder if you'll
ever know
the adventure we never
had.

The Smell of the lemon never leaves

The truth is
you never really leave,
you are always there in some form,

a foreign word
a written sound
a crying sunset
a walking cloud

a simple thought.

The lemons still linger,
it's me and you until
there's no laughs
or love to inhabit these bones.
The sky will sink
and fill again,
others will come
then leave,
littering their scars
on my canvas.
It's how I paint away
these mid-age days.

No matter which colour
I choose to scribe this life,
there will always be a shade
that shows
she was here.

Sahara at 5 am

As the blanket wraps around us
the cold of the night paints
the sky in mystery.
A million dabs of silver dust
dot the ocean overhead
while our bodies rise and fall
to the breath of the sleeping camel
beneath them.

Tonight is the perfect mystery,
alive on a spinning rock
lost in an ocean of
black seas and sands,
an abyss
so large and luminous
the brain can't
understand.

But here we sit

beneath this enigmatic blanket
of blinding grace,
the silence is drowned
by the sound
of birds unknown to my ear
and the whisper of a
river running towards
a midnight grave.

Our hearts beat in rhythm with

the drumroll of the Universe
while our dreams sleep
as still as the shape
of Saharan sand.

Fading

Sat on this black powder beach
watching as you collect shells from the shore
I feel something fade.

The wings of this heart
don't flap the way they used to,
slowed to a stop
like the knees
of an ageing butterfly.

Please fly again
dear
friend
of
mine.

So near So far

We sat on that sofa arm,
strangers yesterday
friends today,
sharing the music of our lives
on that silent Malaysian night.
The only souls awake
while the world around us slept,
Me, you, and the stars
that sang
above.

The walls around us
listened to the music of our hearts,
smiling gently as we joked
away the night.
As I went to bed and
watched as you climbed into yours,
a moonbeam crept through the window
of our room,
smiling
but
crying.

I laid in that pale light and thought only of
you through the early hours,
resting there above me,
a stranger yesterday,
much more today,
So near, yet so far.

Song to You

You are the fabric of the planet.

You are why I carry this rucksack
and roam these roads.

The thieves and the thinkers,
the empty books and the teachers

You are every word in this book
and this body.

Role models aren't always on walls

My favourite photo I ever took was not of
a sight or a sunset, it was a smile.

Worn by a young girl who would walk past my
room
as the sun splintered the Himalayan peaks each
morning.

Her destination was the river,
through the village
down the slopes
past the dried-out mango trees
to the fresh water that rushed
like a ghostly road of second-hand dreams.

3 and a bit miles down and around.

She would fill her bucket with the
liquid of the river and bring it
back up the slope
passed the patch of dying mango trees
through the village
to her home where the family would
wash away the Nepali night.

This was her morning chore,
walk, water, wash all before
the sun had even said its first words.

When I arrived back in London,
I took the bus and sat behind

two men complaining about the pain of the delays
they had faced on their way home from Spain.

I looked out at the well-manicured roads
filled with shiny Vauxhalls and Fords,
and thought of the young girl
on her morning walk,
carrying her bucket of water while
wearing that unscripted smile.

The Welder of Dreams

His Marrakech cave flickered
with the gray stripes of broken TVs,
peering through spectacles
hung low on his old nose,
as white glowed
from this magician's welding rod
adopted from a Spielbergian script.

A mountain of bruised TVs
resting around the walls.
Saturday's life runs by his shop front
but his eyes focus only on
that piercing glow.

A broken TV is like a fractured
doorway to the world
that sits between reality and
the distant land
of colours, characters and contrasts.
He is the gatekeeper,
the locksmith of life,
as a low hiss hums like a
hungover mosquito
in the musky
Moroccan night.

The dreamweaver to us all
working his mysterious ways

as he selotapes our weekend dreams
from deep within his cave.

A Living Disco

I forgot how alive I was for a while
then I met Marrakech. She washed that way of life
back into my blood with the speed of a

sewer rat. Her smoke butterflied through the
square's night air before she had pulled on a

single cigarette. An attack on the eyes, colours
crashing as madness meets man and a donkey
carries a family's living room along the dusty

road. Everyone knows you and where you are
heading before it's entered your own head, there's a
man whose hand reaches inside a cow's corpse,
while next door an elderly woman bakes Arabic

bread, cats who cuddle under bins to hide from
bikes that feast on the city's bones, an Octopus's
idea of a map gone wrong. Souks and guides
acrobats and lights, the best friend you never met
hunts you down from either side.

It is sarcasm and summer mixed in a pot of paint
which no brush will fit. If you ever forget how alive
life can really be take a step in Marrakech and taste
the stories on her streets.

One Night in Calais

A message came through from
a soul in hope of a sleeping bag
to fight the February night.

We drove and delivered what we could find,
a bag sent from the kindness of an unknown home.

He smiled in the passenger seat of
our heated Ford,
then stepped outside with bag
in hand,
masked in his beautiful
Sudanese smile.

Walking into the distance
carrying his shadow by his side,
as the jungle's streetlights flickered
and the outline of his despair grew against the
night.

We drove back to the safety of our shelter
and
I lay looking at the window,
that looked out to a world
I could not understand.

The only word that came to me while I tried to
write this poem was

Why?

Whose prison?

While a polar bear slumps
in a cage
sniffing at the 4 inch thick walls
of his German glass jail,
a man whose life appears to
be an Antarctic winter itself
looks into the cage from
a box of his own.

The bear sits in solitude
yet the man sits in wonder,
watching what lives
on another part of the planet

perhaps to
forget what is
alive
on
his
own.

An Ode to an Island

Waves carve their names
across the Eastern shore,
while rivers as blue as
the breaking of young love
flood the torso of this island.

Typhoon damaged skin
stretches on the bones
of islanders
as tough and true
as the ground from which they grew.

Tofu invades the Taipei air
choking my foreign lungs,
enticing theirs.

Motorised flies zip around
the green circus tent
as trees and plants pray
towards the way the wind swept.

Dancing emerald heads on
scaled trapeze poles
line the distinction between
water and coast.

A new friend is never far away
in this jigsaw of past and peace
they could be passing by in a car
or singing their rhythm on a leaf.

It is limestone and lemons,
rotten gums and friendly eyes,
red rivers, hallucinogenic waterfalls
and drunken rollercoaster rides.

Incense sticks burn while the sun wakes
and the stars rest, up and out into the
canvas of clouds, in puffs and pulls,

up and out

out and up

like the death of a dragon.

The Tree that Feeds time (For Gorkha)

There was a tree that stood
so gently perched upon that hill
sat beneath her emerald leaves
it seemed like time stood still.

As children climbed her branches
collecting up her leaves,
passing village women shaded
beneath her jaded greens.

The school bell rang and smiling kids
would run straight for her path,
to spend the evening chasing fireflies
beside her bark.

I wonder if that same old tree still sleeps
there as I write,
is Sitaram sat there singing
to the star-filled Nepali night?

Is that gentle wind of mountain air
still rushing through her roots?
Do the flaming reds of love and life
still glow inside her fruit?

There was a tree that stood
so gently perched upon that hill,
That tree sleeps in my memories
and grows beside me still.

Song to the Unwritten Road

She is my favourite question mark

keeping all of her answers
inside her handbag,
with a little sweat and sacrifice
she let's you look inside.

She is possibilities through perseverance,
ambition and aims.

Perhaps like no other,
She is yours to use as you wish.

I hope I use her well.

A Peculiar Place To Live and Die

Airports are strange beings,
people coming
going
kissing
crying,
coffee cups crushed and
flowers thrown,
loved ones smile as
the face of family
appears from a gate
and then the long
goodbye
begins again.

One day
that gate
won't open,
the face won't appear,
so embrace those faces you love.
The way your eyes hold a conversation
with no words,
the way fingers sing in silence as they
fill your hollow skin.

Airports are strange beings for sure,
but to sit and watch one work
is to watch the world slowly spin

Gently living
Gently dying.

Unsung words from a Wonderful Us

Looking out across Cardiff Bay today
I see the world in the blink of an eye,
Agatanamori park sleeps beside me
with her blossoming branches of Spring,
Bromo and Bandung sit behind
those distant hills,
a ruler's length on a map,
the width of a beating
heart in my head.

Everything at once.

The movie plays on repeat.

She sleeps in her Himalayan home
while I write from my new nest
of uncertain bones.

My friend paints a postcard
on a palm tree isle
while Welsh daisies
form choirs around the
silent path.

My grandfather lays in the arms
of life,
Raging
Raging
against that dying light

and I wonder

where's the line?

That boundary
between the here and now,
the years that surfed before
and those that lay in wait,
asleep on a timeline of our lives
dreaming of yesterdays.

An album of memories and mayhem
lay just over those hills

as the seagulls sing of past fires
I wonder what time will bring.

Us

These 4 walls whisper words of the world
of what could really be,
when we stop, think, and realise our fragility.

A landscape where hugs are given for free,
smiles are donated by every face daily,
to say 'I love you' is as commonplace as
 accepting every person no matter religion or race.

Our blood is always red
our hearts always thirst
to be loved and shown
by family and friends
that they would put you first.

Community and neighbours
You and Me become
We and Us,
every mountain peak is navigable
when love crushes all ifs and buts.

I'll hold your hand through the rushing river
I'll carry you when your legs become old
I'll share with you my final drop
of ambition, happiness and hope.

Born from the same particle of moon dust
branches of the same tree
If I fail, you fail
If you cry, I cry
If you fall

I'll share my dream.

These 4 walls whisper words of the world
of what could really be,
when we start to realise we are the human in

humanity.

Wasted Time

So many are wasting time
thinking back about wasted times,
hindsight can turn a
brick into a bird
a worm into a world,
memories are a fence to the
feast outside.
A padlock to the past
where pastures seemed green
and faces bled with love and laughs.

No more losing time
thinking back about losing times,
those days were as real as
the wrinkles on a snake,
as sharp as the sound of stardust.
I swam a sea for 6 years
and another ocean will follow,
a cap yesterday can be a
crown tomorrow.

No more missing time
thinking back about missed times,
my socks had holes years ago
and today my big toe still shows,
beaten and calloused like a
bruised bird's wing
but this skin is the story,
every cell tells a sentence
each freckle holds a failure

but I barely feel
like I've turned the first page.

No more wasting time
thinking back about wasted times.

There's a world of words to learn and write,
and this body filled with ink
has just begun
its opening line …

Eyes beyond Roath

There are nights when I look
out across the roofs of Roath
and see it all.

The face of that Indonesian shop seller,
The fragrance of a Balinese flower,
That house in Ghorka,
standing like a cookie on crutches.
The electric towers that tickled
Malaysia at midnight,
the waves that sang
to a Sicilian shore
as a dragon slept out back.

A lonely bubble
in a fish filled tank.

An onlooker to life
whose search for words
won't let him swim against the tides,
whose want of understanding
is never fully satisfied.

I guess, there lies the magic.
Watching as the sea pushes
its way towards home,
as we fight against the current
in search of a
mystery of our
own.

Live Forever

I write these lines in an attempt to remember,
worried that one day all those faces, feelings
and photos will be nothing but raindrops in an
empty well, only to find that when I begin,
there's no real way to express the reality of those
times and travels.

Either I'm a failed writer or a man who lived too
much and listened too little. There's a romance in
both. I only hope that those roads walked live
inside me til I'm gone.

Either way, there've been enough days filled with
fireworks to fill 10 Saharan skies

so I leave it up to you

to never let
us or this
die.

These Cream Boots of Mine

These soles have kissed volcano cones
and sipped from Asian rains
conquered the dragon Krakatau,
kissed her Cherry flames.

They've slept on Borneon rocks,
leapt from waterfalls
they've tread through Angkor's temples
and slept on Java's shores.

They've danced in Bali's Reggae bars
and rapped on Emerald stages,
they've walked the Burmese Paradise
and stomped the Oz Oasis.

Walked on Vaci boulevard
ran from Orangutans.
Scarred cafes in Vienna
climbed the Giant in Japan.

They've been to friend's funerals
and swam in teenage tears,
they've warmed my feet when hope was broke
grown stronger through the years.

Found love in Indonesia
put smiles in every thought
but what my creme boots love most
is there's so much more road to walk.

Beyond those hills

Grass as green as the Dragon's garden sets the
stage for Cardiff's spring,

students filled with the syrup of youth, smoke as
the river whispers beside their fading ash.

Cherry blossoms who survived yesterday's winds
rest on their bed of branches. The streets who have
written my story feel close as friends share food
over newly lit flames.

Last year the Japanese Hanami danced inside a sky
of pink petals on this day, but now, here I am,
watching Wales paint the sky purple with a poem
titled 'home'.

A word turned into an enigma through the eyes of
a traveller who now knows there's no boundary
between where your garden starts and the outside
ends.

It's yours.

From the blades of grass in the background
to the grey bricks of The Great Wall,

so if I could share one word with the world
it would have to be

Explore.

Printed in Poland
by Amazon Fulfillment
Poland Sp. z o.o., Wrocław

58465821R00066